THE ASSURANCE OF FAITH
The Firm Foundation of Christian Hope

"They that trust in Jehovah are as Mount Zion, which cannot be moved, but abideth forever." Psalm 125:1

by

LOUIS BERKHOF

Solid Ground Christian Books
Birmingham, Alabama
2004

SOLID GROUND CHRISTIAN BOOKS
PO Box 660132, Vestavia Hills, AL 35266
205-443-0311
sgcb@charter.net
http://www.solid-ground-books.com

The Assurance of Faith:
The Firm Foundation of Christian Hope

by Louis Berkhof

From the 1939 edition by *W.B. Eerdmans Pub. Co., Grand Rapids, MI*

Published by Solid Ground Christian Books

Classic Reprints Series

First printing of paperback edition September 2004

ISBN: 1-932474-52-8

Special thanks to Ric Ergenbright who gave kind permission to use the beautiful photograph that graces the cover of this book. It is with a great deal of gratitude that we have listed his titles and contact information on one of the back pages of this book.

Manufactured in the United States of America

Dedicated to the Memory of One who was

A Faithful Helpmeet

A Loving Mother

A Child of God

PREFACE

This little book is born of the conviction that the subject of the assurance of faith deserves more attention that it often receives in the present day. We are not living in an age in which Christian certitude can be taken for granted. The enemy is exerting himself to destroy the foundation which God has laid for our faith in his excellent Word. Doubts respecting the most fundamental truths of the Bible are rampant everywhere and are also making inroads in the Church of Jesus Christ. Question-marks are fast taking the place of positive assertions of the truth. Such an atmosphere is not conducive to the assurance of salvation, but threatens to rob the Christian of this precious gem. If it ever was necessary to cultivate the assurance of faith, it is necessary to-day, for without it the present generation of Christians will not be equal to the tremendous task that rests upon its shoulders, "to contend earnestly for the faith which was once for all delivered unto the saints," and to guard the good thing that was committed unto it. It is hoped that this little treatise may be of some service in the cultivation of assurance especially among our rising generation. Older catechumens might peruse it with profit. Perhaps it could be used as a gift to those who are making their public profession of faith.

L. BERKHOF

Grand Rapids, Mich.
December, 1938.

TABLE OF CONTENTS

I

THE ASSURANCE OF FAITH

The Question of Assurance in the Present Day

THERE are some subjects that have a perennial appeal for all serious-minded Christians. And among these the subject of the assurance of faith or of salvation occupies an outstanding place. When our preachers address their churches on that vital topic, they may be sure of a goodly number of interested hearers, who are anxious for a description of the foundation of their hope, and who long for a word that will help them to obtain that blessed assurance and will thus fill their hearts with the joy of salvation.

It is true that many professing Christians to-day will not subscribe to this sentiment. In their estimation one who undertakes to speak or write on the subject of assurance is hopelessly behind the time and altogether out of tune with the present trend of religious thought. They do not all formulate their objections in the same way, but they all agree in the desire to ignore or at least, to soft-pedal the question of assurance.

Some emphasize the fact that the character of the Christian battle has changed and the battleground has been shifted. Time was when the Bible was accepted as the infallible Word of God and Bible truths were taken at their face value. Whatever doubts were entertained concerned one's being in a state of grace. The battle was fought single-handed in the citadel of the heart. But now the trustworthiness of the Bible is called in question and even the great verities of faith, such as the incarnation, the virgin birth, the physical resurrection of Jesus Christ, and his physical return in glory, are not only doubted but boldly denied. This calls for a battle in the open field, in which all those who recognize Jesus Christ as their Lord should stand shoulder to shoulder. The struggle to maintain the fundamentals of the Christian religion is so all-absorbing that it really leaves no time for the question of personal assurance. Far more important issues are at stake and must be settled before this question can really mean anything.

In the camp of the Modernists the assertion is repeatedly made that the whole question of personal assurance, which had a proper place in the sixteenth century system of thought, does not fit in at all with the advanced thinking of the present age. There is no supernatural work of God, there are no miracles of grace; why, then, should man anxiously inquire, whether he has experienced a supernatural change? All men are by nature children of God; but if this is true, there is no sense in asking, whether I am one of the favored ones. Salvation is not a gift, but a social achievement of man; therefore the proper thing to do is, not to inquire into the probable reception of the gift, but to engage in works of social reform, in order to change the world into a Kingdom of God.

Moreover, the advocates of the social gospel take great delight in posing as the representatives of a superior ethical code. They claim to have learned the important lesson of subordinating their personal interests to those of society. In their work of social reform they are forgetful of self; egotism has made place for altruism. And from their higher point of view they regard the question of personal assurance as purely selfish, and therefore unworthy of one living in this social age. Men ought to be less concerned about themselves and more about others. If they only do their duty by their fellow-men, the future will take care of itself.

What shall we say to these things? . . . It is perfectly true that conditions have greatly changed since the days of the Reformation. There is today a battle that centers about the Word of God and the great verities of faith as never before. And it would be a great mistake for Christians to concern themselves only about their personal assurance and to lose sight of the more fundamental battle. What value has personal assurance, if the Bible is not dependable? It presupposes the truth of Scripture. Therefore the very desire for the assurance of salvation should prompt those who seek it to fight the forces of unbelief.

But, on the other hand, their battle for the Bible should not cause them to lose sight of the question of assurance. They ought not to think for a moment that they can safely ignore this in view of the greater issues that are now at stake. The Reformers certainly did not take that attitude. They too had to contend earnestly for the faith once delivered to the saints, but never ceased to stress the necessity of personal assurance. In fact, it may be said that they occasionally overshot the mark in this respect. But it is exactly because they were so tremendously in earnest about this assurance, that they were able to perform their herculean task. May it not be that the Christians of to-day are so weak in comparison, just because they do not stress this important matter?

Again, it is true that the question of personal assurance, at least in the form in which it is generally put, has no meaning in the system of thought that is widely prevalent in scientific circles to-day. But this is no reason why serious-minded Christians should not pay just as much attention to it as ever before. They who accept the Bible as the ultimate standard of truth surely ought not to commit the folly of allowing the vagaries of Modernism to dominate their Christian life. There is indeed a danger that the prevailing mode of thought will cause them to disregard the question of the assurance of salvation. Unless they are very much on their guard, they will naturally come under the influences of the spirit of the age in this respect. The very opposition it calls forth may divert their attention from the strengthening of the inner life, and cause them to resemble those churches that are abundant in missionary efforts, but meanwhile neglect the home base.

But is it not really selfish to pay so much attention to personal assurance? There are some well-meaning Christians who, in spite of themselves, are inclined to think that the charge is true, and are therefore rather hesitant to speak about this assurance. But the objection is really absurd. The underlying assumption would seem to be that all attention to self with a view to its welfare, is selfish. It is a patent fact, however, that the Modernist himself does not believe that, for then he would also have to consider eating and drinking, hygienic measures, physical exercise, the cultivation of moral purity, etc., as thoroughly selfish, and yet these are the very things that are stressed by the social gospel. It is certainly no more selfish to cultivate spiritual, than it is to promote physical well-being. Of course, it is possible for one to be so neglectful of other duties in seeking the assurance of faith, and to have the eye so exclusively fixed on salvation as a desirable future, as to expose oneself to the charge of selfishness. But seeking personal assurance is not in itself an evidence of selfishness. We may be seeking our spiritual well-being in this respect, in order that we may be more able to help others, to promote the cause of God, to reveal the glory of his grace, and to magnify Him for the riches of the inheritance which He has prepared for us. Moreover, we should not forget that God himself demands of us that we be diligent unto the full assurance of hope unto the end; and that He certainly would not require of us what is morally reprehensible.

The treatment of this subject, then, does not call for an apology. On the contrary, there are good reasons for discussing it. There are comparatively few Christians to-day, who really glory in the assurance of salvation. The note of heavenly joy seems to have died away out of the life of God's people. It is true that it may sometimes be heard in Methodist revival meetings. But in such cases it is generally prompted only by momentary emotions, often proves to be of an evanescent character, and is frequently followed by reactions of the darkest gloom. Moreover, the assurance in which the Methodist glories always falls short of the assurance of salvation.

There are always large numbers of serious seekers after assurance in our churches, who are tossed to and fro by doubts and uncertainties. Some of them appear to be chronic doubters, who occasionally create the impression that they take a secret delight in their doubts and regard them as a mark of special piety. But the majority are of a different kind. They can readily be made to understand that the normal Christian life cannot be one of constant uncertainty, and that their doubts are due to a certain measure of unbelief, to weakness of faith, or to ignorance, and therefore cannot be condoned. As a rule they are in a teachable spirit, eager to receive instruction and help, and anxious to be led into the light. They need careful spiritual guidance and should always be the objects of tender solicitude.

But we also meet with some professing Christians to-day—and it is to be feared that their number is on the increase—who apparently do not think about the matter of assurance, or who, if they do, fail to take it seriously. They simply seem to take it for granted, and speak of it as a matter of course. They assert their assurance in an off-hand way, but leave the impression that they hardly know what it means. It is quite evident that the matter of personal assurance has not gripped their souls. Their spiritual life moves on the surface and is utterly lacking in real depth. In view of all this it can hardly be called superfluous to call attention to this important subject.

II

THE DOCTRINE OF ASSURANCE
IN HISTORY

a. *At the Time of the Reformation*

THE Reformers rejoiced in the assurance of salvation as a tower of strength. This Christian certitude made them irresistible in their attacks on the church of Rome and adamant in resisting the onslaughts of the enemy. They were the first to place the doctrine of assurance, which they regarded as a precious jewel, prominently in the foreground; the first also to impress upon the people the necessity of personal assurance. This was one of their most important points of departure from the church that claimed to be the only ark of safety, and yet was totally unable to engender a feeling of security in the hearts of those that sought shelter in it. Augustine had already called attention to the fact that faith included assurance as to its objects, certainty respecting the objective truths of revelation. And because Roman Catholic theologians generally took the same position, the Reformer found no occasion to differ from them on that score. The situation was quite different, however, in the matter of personal assurance. The prevailing tendency was to deny that this was in any sense included in what was called "the assurance of faith."

Some of the schoolmen, who accepted the tenets of Semi-Pelagianism, had already denied the possibility of the assurance of salvation, and in doing this could claim the merit of consistency. Their view of the matter gradually gained the upper hand in the Roman Catholic church and was finally formulated by the Council of Trent. It declared that the assurance of being in a state of grace and of final salvation is impossible, except by some special revelation. The position of the church of Rome is that such a revelation is enjoyed by very few, perhaps only by the martyr-saints. The great majority of believers must be satisfied with a mere moral probability.

This doctrine of perennial uncertainty respecting the highest interests of life is the natural consequence of the Semi-Pelagian doctrine of sin and grace, and of the practice of the church of Rome to make the forgiveness of sin largely dependent on the sacrament of penance and on the ministrations of a human intermediary. The Roman Catholic does not believe in the total depravity of man, and therefore cannot infer from the sparks of a higher life within himself, that God has begun the work of redemption. He looks upon faith primarily as a work of man, a mere assent to the truth accepted by the church, and not as a gift of divine grace, a trustful resting on the Saviour. Moreover, his faith is not directed altogether away from himself to the mercy of God revealed in

Jesus Christ, the same yesterday, to-day, and forever, but is made to rest, at least in part, on the uncertain foundation of his own moral state, and on the good works which he accomplishes. Neither does he accept the doctrine of an absolute predestination, and the resulting truths, that the grace of God works only in the elect, and that by this grace the saints will persevere unto the end. He feels that even a present state of grace does not yet guarantee final salvation.

Moreover, the Roman Catholic church makes the forgiveness of sins dependent, not on an immediate divine act of pardon once for all, but on the sacrament of penance that must be repeated after every mortal sin, and on the absolution of the priest. With every new deadly sin the state of grace is lost. It can only be restored by the sacrament of penance, and is lost again whenever a new mortal sin is committed. But this is not the only thing that makes assurance impossible. The confessional itself is hedged about with all kinds of uncertainties. The orders of the functioning priest may not be genuine, and this would make his absolution ineffectual. His intention may be at fault, and this would introduce another element of uncertainty. Then, too, the confessor may be ambiguous, equivocal, or indeterminate. He may overlook some of his sins and fail to mention them to the priest, in which case they would not be forgiven. It is no wonder therefore that, according to the church at Rome, the assurance of salvation is quite out of the question.

But the Roman Catholic church even goes a step farther: it regards personal assurance as undesirable. The real reason for this is, in all probability, that the church greatly profits by keeping the souls of the faithful in constant suspense. It reaps a rich harvest through the sacrament of penance. Of course, it does not assign this as a reason for its teaching on this point. It claims to consider it wholesome and beneficial for the Christian to entertain honest doubts in the high matters of justification and final salvation. Such doubts keep him from an overweening confidence in himself, minister to true humility of character, and serve as a more salutary restraint on the evil passions than joy and peace in believing could ever be. Möhler, one of the greatest Roman Catholic scholars of the previous century said: "I think that, in the neighborhood of any man, who would declare himself under all circumstances assured of his salvation, I should feel very uncomfortable, and should probably have difficulty to put away the thought, that something like diabolical influence was here at play."

The Reformers with their emphasis on the doctrines of divine election, the total inability of man to do any spiritual good and to turn to God with a penitent heart, man's absolute dependence on the grace of God only for salvation, his justification by faith and not by the works of the law, and the perseverance of the saints—naturally took an entirely different position. In connection with the question of assurance the leading topic of discussion between them and the Catholics was at first simply whether, without any special revelation, believers could and should be assured of their justification and salvation. The Catholics denied, and the Reformers affirmed this. And on this point orthodox Protestant divines concurred with them ever since.

This is not the precise form, however, which the controversy finally assumed. The Roman Catholics gradually led it into a different channel. Some of the more reasonable among them did not dare to meet the question in its original form with a direct negative. They preferred to discuss the kind or the degree of assurance ordinarily attainable by believers. Thus the Reformers were led into a discussion of the nature and the grounds of Christian certitude. They claimed that the assurance possible was of the highest and most perfect description, a certainty like that with which men believe the plainly revealed truths of Scripture; that it was necessarily involved in justifying faith, was its distinguishing characteristic, and in fact belonged to its very essence.

Both Luther and Calvin used some very strong expressions on this point, expressions which seem to imply that one who lacks personal assurance cannot be regarded as a true believer, and that one having true faith cannot entertain doubts respecting his final salvation. Says Calvin: "We shall now have a full definition of faith if we say that it is a firm and sure knowledge of the divine favour toward us, founded on the truth of a free promise in Christ, and revealed to our minds, and sealed on our hearts, by the Holy Spirit." And again: "No man," I say, "is a believer but who, trusting to the security of his salvation, confidently triumphs over the devil and death." At the same time it is clear that he did not mean to teach that true believers never battle with doubts and uncertainties. Says he: "When we inculcate that faith ought to be certain and secure, we conceive not of a certainty attended with no doubt, or of a security interrupted by no anxiety; but rather affirm that believers have a perpetual conflict with their own diffidence, and are far from placing their consciences in a placid calm never disturbed by any storms." He evidently intends to teach that, though faith contains and always retains the element of assurance, the believer does not always so exercise faith that he is constantly free from doubts and perplexities. In other words, that the sense, the feeling of assurance, increases and decreases with the rise and decline in the exercises of faith.

b. *In the Confessional Period*

If we turn to our Confessional Standards, we find that the Heidelberg Catechism also takes the position that assurance is of the very essence of faith. Its classic reply to the question, "What is true faith?" is well known. "It is not only a certain knowledge whereby I hold for truth all that God has revealed to us in his Word, but also a hearty trust which the Holy Ghost works in me by the Gospel, that not only to others, but to me also, forgiveness of sins, everlasting righteousness and salvation, are freely given by God, merely of grace, only for the sake of Christ's merits."

This answer of the Catechism can be traced back to the Smaller Catechism of Ursinus, which, in turn, is dependent on his Larger Catechism. In the former we read: "Faith is a strong assent by which we accept all that is revealed to us in the Word of God; and a sure confidence created by the Holy Spirit in the hearts of God's elect, whereby each one feels assured that, through the merits of Christ alone, remission of sins, righteousness and eternal life are freely given by God, only for the merits of Christ." This answer, as was said, may again be traced back to the Larger Catechism: "Faith is a firm assent to every Word of God, and a firm confidence, by which every one holds that forgiveness of sin, righteousness and eternal life are given him by God, freely, on account of the merits of Christ; and through confidence is an illumination in the hearts of the elect by the Holy Spirit, making us living members of Christ and producing in us true love of God and prayer."

There can be no doubt as to the standpoint of the Catechism on the question of assurance. It is even more evident from Ursinus' Commentary on the Heidelberg Catechism, edited by his pupil, David Paraeus, which states that, where this confidence is not found, but rather distrust, despair, or constant doubt, there is no true saving faith; and declares it to be certain that they who believe also know that they believe. Moreover, it is perfectly clear that the Catechism's emphasis on the assurance of faith is in

harmony with the general tenor of its teachings, and
that it was determined by its opposition to the doctrine of the church of Rome. Over against the
Roman Catholic idea that religion is fear, the Heidelberg Catechism sounds the joyous note that religion
is a comfort. Its keynote is found in the precious
answer to the first question, "What is thy only comfort in life and death?" "That I with body and
soul, both in life and in death, am not my own, but
belong to my faithful Saviour Jesus Christ, who with
his precious blood has fully satisfied for all my sins,
and redeemed me from all the power of the devil;
and so preserves me that without the will of my
Father in heaven not a hair can fall from my head;
yea that all things must work together for my salvation. Wherefore by his Holy Spirit He also assures me of eternal life, and makes me heartily willing and ready henceforth to live unto Him." This
note of personal assurance, sounded in the very first
answer, recurs time and again, as appears from the
following questions and answers: 21, 26, 28, 32, 39,
44, 52, 54, etc. Faith clearly stands forth as a trustful reliance on, an appropriation of Christ as the
Mediator given of God, and as such carries with it a
certitude that fills the heart with the joy of salvation.

The Canons of Dort were framed in opposition
to the Arminians, who moved in the direction of
Rome without going to the same extreme. They
granted the possibility of the assurance of being in
a present state of grace, but denied that believers
could be sure of their future salvation without a spe-

cial revelation, and held that such assurance in believers generally would only lead to carnal security,
and would be highly detrimental to a truly pious and
holy life. On the other hand the Canons of Dort
maintain that believers can, in their present life, obtain the assurance of their future salvation, and that
they actually enjoy this assurance *according to the
measure of their faith*. This would seem to imply that
Christian certitude is of the essence of saving faith.
They further assert that this assurance does not result from any special revelation, but is based on the
promises of God in his Word, on the testimony of
the Holy Spirit in the hearts of believers, and on the
exercise of a good conscience and the production of
good works as the fruits of faith. It is admitted
that believers are not always conscious of this full
assurance of faith and this certainty of persevering
to the end, since this may be obscured by doubts and
uncertainties; but it is also maintained that out of
these spiritual struggles faith will again rise trium-
phantly to the height of assurance. Moreover, this
assurance is regarded as highly desirable, since it
does not minister to pride and carnal security, but
is rather a source of humility, filial reverence, true
piety, patience in tribulation, constancy in suffering
and confessing the truth, and of solid rejoicing in
God.

The Westminster Confession apparently sounds
a different note, when it says: "This infallible assurance doth not so belong to the essence of faith, but
that a true believer may wait long, and conflict with

many difficulties before he be a partaker of it: yet, being enabled by the Spirit to know the things that are freely given him of God, he may, without extraordinary revelation, in the right use of ordinary means, attain thereunto." Presbyterian divines generally interpret this to mean that, though faith carries with it a certainty respecting the truth of the promises of salvation in Christ, it does not include what is usually called "the assurance of salvation," or "the assurance of hope," i.e. the personal assurance of being in a state of grace, of having a saving interest in Jesus Christ, and of being an heir of everlasting life. But it is possible to put a different interpretation on the words of the Confession, as was done by the Marrow-men, who were accused in 1720 of teaching contrary to the doctrine of the Confession that assurance is of the essence of faith. It should be noted that the Confession speaks of a complex assurance, resting in part on the promises of God, and in part on the evidence of the inward graces wrought in the life of believers and the testimony of the Holy Spirit. It calls this the "infallible (full) assurance of faith," and asserts that this is not necessarily enjoyed by believers from the very moment that they accept Christ by faith. So understood the teaching of the Confession does not materially differ from that of the Reformers and of the other great Protestant Confessions, though there is undoubtedly a difference of emphasis. It may also be regarded as significant that the Confession, speaking of faith, says: "This faith is different in degrees, weak or strong; may be often and many ways assailed and weakened, but gets the victory; *growing up in many to the attainment of a full assurance* through Christ, who is both the author and finisher of our faith." How can faith grow into this full assurance, if assurance is not, in any sense, of the essence of faith? Moreover, the Confession also takes the position that, though believers may have the assurance of their salvation divers ways shaken, diminished, and intermitted, "yet they are never utterly destitute of that seed of God . . . out of which, by the operation of the Holy Spirit, this assurance may in due time be revived, and by the which, in the meantime, they are supported from utter despair." We fully agree with Shaw, when he says in his Commentary on the Confession: "But although the assurance described in this chapter (the full assurance referred to above) is not essential to faith, yet there is an assurance which belongs to the essence of faith, and this our Confession recognizes in the Chapter which treats of saving faith."

c. *In the Last Two Centuries*

In the eighteenth century the religious life of Europe suffered from the blight of Rationalism. Religion became a matter of the intellect only, and religious truth was made to depend on rational arguments. Religious certainty was identified with a rational insight into the truth, and divorced from the experience of a supernatural change, and the resulting testimony of the Holy Spirit. Under this chilling

influence real spiritual life fast declined, and alongside of it there appeared a luxurious growth of a
purely historical or a merely temporal faith.

It was but natural that reaction should follow.
When a spurious faith became alarmingly prevalent,
the question forced itself upon serious-minded Christians with an ever increasing insistency: How can
we distinguish the true from the false? The proper
method was found in a close and sustained self-
examination. The life of the soul was submitted to a
very careful scrutiny and to an analysis surprising in
its minuteness. A constantly growing number of
marks were discovered by which true faith might be
recognized, many of them based on an unwarranted
generalization and therefore of a very questionable
character. The spiritual experiences of those who
were regarded as established Christians became the
standard by which others were judged. But, though
this method was undoubtedly applied with the best
intention, it did not promote the glad assurance of
salvation in the Church of God; in many cases it
even led to hopeless confusion. Perplexing doubts
and uncertainties became so common that even these
were finally looked upon as a mark of true piety.
Scripture warrant for this was found in the word of
Solomon, "Happy is the man that feareth alway,"
Prov. 28:14. A distinction was made between the
being and the well-being of faith; between a faith
merely fleeing for refuge to Christ and an assured
faith. The general conviction was that assurance
was not of the essence or of the very being of faith,

and was certainly not included in any sense in a faith that merely revealed itself in a fleeing to Christ for salvation. Assurance was, in fact, regarded as a high and rare privilege, the prerogative of a few favored souls, sometimes obtained only in a special way.

There is especially one great historical movement that sought to point out a more excellent way to obtain personal assurance. Methodism reacted against the prevailing spiritual pessimism of the age and aimed at promoting a cheerful and joyous Christian life. And this is still one of its purposes to-day. It places the sinner squarely before the law of God and causes him to tremble at the thought of the coming judgment. But when it has cast him down, has filled his heart with the terrors of the law, and has brought him to a realization of his lost condition, it at once gladdens the heart with the joyous message of salvation. The experience of salvation is contracted in a single moment; the deepest gloom is instantly transformed into the greatest joy. And it is only natural that this tremendous change immediately carries with it a full assurance. The converted sinner at once shouts for joy, because he feels that he is saved. This glad assurance Methodism regards as one of the characteristics of saving faith.

Now it may strike us as an anomaly that the Methodist can feel sure of being saved from the very moment of his conversion, and at the same time deny the doctrines of election, of the irresistible character of the grace of God, and of the perseverance of the saints. But this apparent inconsistency disappears, if we bear in mind that his assurance pertains to the present only and not the future, that it is an assurance of being in a present state of grace, and not an assurance of final salvation. Wesley describes this assurance as the result of an immediate operation of the Holy Spirit; but there is no small danger that it will ultimately prove to be only a psychological effect, artificially produced by playing on the emotions. Moreover, Sheldon, himself a Methodist, is quite correct in saying: "Wesley's description of the Holy Spirit's agency, as consisting in the immediate production of a specific conviction, applies far better to a possible crisis or exceptional exigency in Christian experience than to assurance as a standing fact in the normal Christian life." With the Methodist assurance is almost exclusively a matter of the feelings, and is therefore a rather unstable thing in itself. The assurance that reveals itself in the shouts of joy that are heard in present day revivals is not a very dependable thing. It easily turns into a feeling of great depression, and even of utter despair.

III

THE CONNECTION BETWEEN FAITH
AND ASSURANCE

a. *The Question at Issue*

FROM the preceding pages it is perfectly clear that Protestants have not always been entirely unanimous on the subject of assurance. They are not all in full agreement to-day. Even among Reformed theologians there is considerable difference of opinion as to whether assurance belongs to the very essence of faith, so that he who truly believes in Jesus Christ unto salvation always has a certain measure of assurance; or whether it is merely one of the fruits of faith, and a fruit that may not appear until years after one has accepted Christ as his Saviour. Hence the question arises, Does the very act of believing, of accepting Christ in true faith, involve a certain measure of assurance or not?

In any attempt to answer this question it ought to be clearly understood just what the term assurance implies in this connection. The prevalent expression "assurance of faith" is rather ambiguous. It may denote any one of three or four things, but it may also be used in a comprehensive sense, so as to include all its special meanings. There is, first of all, what is often called "the assurance of assent to the

33

truth." It is grounded in the acceptance of the Bible as the infallible Word of God, and consists in the conviction that Christ is all that He is represented to be, and that the blessed promises of the Gospel are absolutely reliable. No one will be inclined to doubt that this assurance belongs to the essence of faith. It is found even in faith in its most general sense, for this is exactly the acceptance of something as true on the basis of the testimony of another. It naturally involves a conviction respecting the truth of that which is accepted. Such a conviction is also included in saving faith, as even the Roman Catholics will admit. But though some would limit the meaning of the term "assurance of faith" to this bare intellectual assent to the truth, it is not generally so restricted. In fact, this certitude respecting the object of faith is not what is ordinarily called the assurance of faith. Yet it is closely connected with it, and is in fact fundamental for any farther assurance. No one who doubts the Scriptural representation of the Gospel of Jesus Christ can have any personal assurance of salvation. They who assume a critical attitude with respect to the revealed truths of Scripture and yet glory in the certainty of their redemption, are deceiving themselves. The one excludes the other. Ultimately personal assurance can only be rooted in a hearty acceptance of Jesus Christ, as He is set forth in the Gospel, and in a conviction of the truth of the Gospel promises.

There is also, in the second place, what has been called the "assurance of application or appropriation," which, in the language of Scripture is called a reliance on God and on Jesus Christ, a trusting in Him and in the word of his grace unto salvation. It is the appropriating persuasion of faith, whereby we embrace the promises of God and Jesus Christ himself, in whom they are yea and amen; apply these promises to ourselves, accepting Jesus Christ as our personal Saviour, and thus appropriate whatever is offered in the word of promise and in the righteousness of him who gave his life for sinners. This means that, where God comes to us in his divine Word with the promise of the forgiveness of sins, of the perfect righteousness in Jesus Christ, and of eternal life in communion with God, we believingly accept the promise and enter into the riches of grace that are freely given us of God, thus becoming "heirs of God and joint-heirs with Christ." This assurance consists therefore in a *personal* appropriation of the general promises of the Gospel. It finds beautiful expression in these words of the Catechism, in which the believer gives an explication of his faith in God the Father: "That the eternal Father of our Lord Jesus Christ . . . is for the sake of Christ His Son, my God and my Father; on whom I rely so entirely, that I have no doubt, that He will provide me with all things necessary for soul and body: and farther, that He will make whatever evil He sends upon me in this valley of tears turn out to my advantage; for He is able to do it, being Almighty God, and willing also, being a faithful Father."

Finally, there is a third kind of assurance, an assurance that does not terminate on the promises of God, but on the spiritual state of the believer. It does not look to that which is objectively given in the Word of God, but rather to that which is subjectively wrought in the heart of the Holy Spirit. It is frequently called the assurance of sense, as resting upon the inward sense the soul has of the reality of its spiritual experiences. Some theologians restrict the use of the term "assurance of faith" to the objective assurance of the truth of the promises, of which we have spoken in the preceding, and prefer to speak of the assurance now under consideration as the "assurance of hope." It is the firm conviction, based on the evidence of spiritual graces, that the faith we possess is a true and living faith, and that we are indeed children of God. According to the Methodists it embodies a judgment on the state of believers only as far as the present is concerned, but according to the Reformed it has reference to the future as well. It is not merely a certain persuasion that we are now in a state of grace, but also an assurance of future salvation. And this is undoubtedly in harmony with the Scriptural idea of assurance, which makes the future radiant with heavenly light. It prompts the believer to join the apostle in his triumphant strain: "For ye received not the spirit of bondage again to fear; but ye received the spirit of adoption, whereby we cry, Abba, Father. The Spirit himself beareth witness with our spirit, that we are children of God: and if children, then heirs, heirs of God, and joint-heirs with Christ."

Now the question with which we are concerned in this chapter is not, whether a real and living faith involves the conviction that the doctrine of salvation, revealed in the Bible, and all the blessed promises of the Gospel are true. There is no difference of opinion on this point. The question is rather, whether saving faith necessarily includes an element of that subjective personal assurance which engenders a feeling of security and fills the heart with confidence for the future. The Heidelberg Catechism certainly implies that it does; and the Reformers, in their strong opposition to Rome, occasionally used expressions which convey the idea that faith at once carries with it the full joy of salvation. This position is also reflected in the Lambeth Articles of 1595: "A man truly faithful, that is, such a one who is endued with a justifying faith, is certain, with the full assurance of faith, of the remission of his sins and of his everlasting salvation by Christ." On the other hand many Presbyterians deny that saving faith necessarily involves a measure of personal assurance. Jonathan Edwards wrote substantially as follows to Ebenezer Erskine, who was one of the Marrow-men of Scotland and therefore sided with the Reformers: "Faith is belief, in its general sense, of what God has revealed to us in the Gospel. He has revealed to us that all who believe will be saved, and we must believe that on the ground of the Gospel assertion: but He has not revealed to us in the Gospel that I, Jonathon Edwards, of Northampton, shall be saved, and therefore that does not belong to the essence of faith. The essence of faith consists in receiving what God has revealed."

b. *The Assurance That Is Essential to Faith*

Let us turn to the Word of God to see what light it sheds on the point in question. It is abundantly evident from Scripture that faith includes something more than an intellectual conviction concerning the truth of what is contained in the Word of God, and particularly of the way of redemption revealed in Jesus Christ. The Roman Catholics limit it to this, so that faith becomes a mere intellectual assent, without any element of personal assurance. Protestant theology, however, is unanimous in teaching that saving faith also contains an element of trust, and that this is by no means the least important constituent of faith.

The trust-element is very much in the foreground in the Old Testament. It already appears in the word that is fundamental and typical for all Old Testament faith, viz. Gen. 15:6, "And he (Abraham) believed in Jehovah, and He reckoned it to him for righteousness." Here the meaning of the original can best be given as follows: And he developed assurance in, a trustful repose on Jehovah. He caused his soul to rest, not merely on the promises of God, but on God himself. That the Old Testament trusting is the same as the New Testament believing is evident from a comparison of Jer. 17:5, 7 with Heb.

3:12. In the former passage we read: "Cursed is the man that trusteth in man, and maketh flesh his arm, and whose heart departeth from the Lord . . . Blessed is the man that trusteth in the Lord, whose hope the Lord is"; and in the latter: "Take heed, brethren, lest there be in any of you an evil heart of unbelief, in departing from the living God." The two are used as words of the same import in Ps. 78:22, where the Lord complains of the faithlessness of his people, "Because they believed not in God, and trusted not in His salvation." This trusting in the Lord involves security. "They that trust in Jehovah are as mount Zion, which cannot be moved, but abideth forever," Ps. 125:1.

The New Testament, as well as the Old, bears witness to the fact that trust is an essential element in faith. This is strikingly brought out by Christ himself on several occasions. He clearly intimates that a lack of trust either in God or in himself is indicative of a small measure of faith. When the disciples proved to be anxious for food and raiment, He reminded them of God's care for the birds of the air and the lilies of the field, and then added: "But if God so clothe the grass of the field, which to-day is, and to-morrow is cast into the oven, shall He not much more clothe you, *O ye of little faith?*" Matt. 6:30. And when they feared that they would perish in the storm on the Sea of Galilee, He said to them: "Why are ye fearful, *O ye of little faith* (or: *"Have ye not yet faith?"*), Matt. 8:26; Mark 4:40. Again, when Peter at the Lord's command walked upon the waters of the sea, but lost courage and needed a saving hand, he received the rebuke: *"O thou of little faith,* wherefore didst thou doubt?" On the other hand, when the Syro-Phoenician woman revealed implicit trust in the Saviour, she was commended with the word: *"O woman, great is thy faith."* These examples would seem to show very clearly that faith involves a feeling of personal security and safety. Anxiety and doubt, fear and distrust, are attributed to a deficient faith. The proper measure of faith naturally carries with it a feeling of ease, of quietness, and of perfect safety on the stormy sea of life. It inspired the song of the poet: "Jehovah is my light and my salvation: whom shall I fear? Jehovah is the strength of my life; of whom shall I be afraid? . . . I had fainted, unless I had believed to see the goodness of Jehovah in the land of the living. Wait for Jehovah: Be strong, and let thy heart take courage; yea, wait thou for Jehovah."

Now it is perfectly natural that the trust-element in faith should involve a feeling of personal security and safety. To trust is to rely on someone with respect to some vital concern of life. And if this trust be whole-hearted and complete, it will banish all fears, set the mind at rest, and fill the heart with a sense of security. It will enable the believer to join the prophet in his expression of perfect confidence in God: "For though the fig-tree shall not flourish, neither shall fruit be in the vines; the labor of the olive shall fail, and the fields shall yield no food;

the flock shall be cut off from the fold, and there shall be no herd in the stalls: yet I will rejoice in Jehovah, I will joy in the God of my salvation." Hab. 3:17, 18. The child feels perfectly safe on its father's arm, though he carry it through a flood; the warrior feels secure in the strong fortress that is the object of his trust.

> "The child leans on its parent's breast,
> Leaves there its cares, and is at rest.
>
> "The heart that trusts forever sings,
> And feels as light as it had wings;
> A well of peace within it springs."

When we are cast down upon the sickbed, we send for the physician in whom we have confidence, and the measure of our confidence will largely determine the measure in which our fears are dispelled and hope rises within the heart. The same is true in a far higher sense, when we entrust ourselves with our spiritual ills to the great Physician in reliance on his promises. Fear as to our personal safety and our future well-being is not compatible with real trust in him. An undivided heart, that trusts God as it should, is raised above all the anxieties of life. It is sure of the present and sure of the future.

This idea is brought out in Scripture also, where faith is represented as the sure foundation of hope. In fact, hoping in God and hoping in his mercy are sometimes represented as practically equivalent to trusting in God. Thus the poet sings: "Happy is he that hath the God of Jacob for his help, whose hope is in Jehovah his God." Ps. 145:5. And the prophet speaks of Jehovah as "the hope of Israel, and the Saviour thereof in time of trouble." Jer. 14:8. That faith is the very root out of which hope springs, is quite evident from Heb. 11:1, no matter how we render the words. We may read with the Authorized Version, "faith is the substance of things hoped for"; or with the American Revision, "faith is the assurance of things hoped for"; or with Moffat, "faith means we are confident of what we hope for." On every one of these renderings the fact remains that hope is embedded in faith. And each one of them contains a special element of truth. Faith gives present reality to the things of the future, it assures us of the realization of the things hoped for, and it fills the heart with a confident expectation of future bliss. It is characteristic of the writer of the Epistle to the Hebrews that he regards faith particularly as that attitude of the heart and of the mind that would enable the readers to rise above the seen to the unseen, above the present to the future, and to preserve hope amid the disappointments of life. Now faith can be the sure bridge to hope only, because it does not stop at the acceptance of a testimony, but also embraces and thus appropriates a promise.

The basis of the assurance that belongs to the direct action of faith lies in the promises of God; and the classical example of such assurance is found in the case of Abraham. He received a promise that seemed quite impossible of fulfilment. Yet mindful of the power of God, "who giveth life to the dead, and calleth the things that are not, as though they were," he staggered not at the promise. "Looking unto the promise of God, he wavered not through unbelief, but waxed strong through faith, giving glory to God, and being fully assured that what He had promised, He was able also to perform." Abraham did not doubt the promise; neither did he doubt the power or the faithfulness of God. He was sure that he would receive what God had promised him, no matter how impossible it might seem. No wonder that he is represented in Scripture as the exemplary believer.

Right here it may be necessary to meet an objection. It may be said that the promise to Abraham was a personal promise, while the promise of the Gospel is not personal but of a general character: Whosoever believeth in the Lord Jesus Christ shall be saved. This is perfectly true, but we should not forget that, in the very act of faith, the promise becomes personal. Notice the stages by which the believer reaches the confidence of faith. He is first brought to a realization of his own sinful and lost condition. Then the eyes of his understanding are opened to the fact that God in Christ has opened a way of redemption for sinners. This already engenders a feeling of security, and saves him from despondency. There is a Saviour, there is a way of salvation for sinners. In his continued study of the Scriptures he discovers there a picture of the sinner for whom Christ has shed his precious blood, and

soon recognizes this as a description of himself. Thus
the general promise of the Gospel becomes personal
for him; he feels that God comes to him with the
promise of pardon and of eternal bliss. And finally,
he not only believes in the truth of the promise, but
appropriates it and fixes his confidence on Christ as
his personal Saviour.

Thus the direct act of the faith undoubtedly involves an element of assurance. This assurance may
be implicit rather than explicit in the first act of faith,
may not at once reach the level of clear consciousness, and may for a long time be a matter of instinctive feeling rather than of positive knowledge; yet it
is destined to grow, and its growth will be commen-
surate with the measure of faith. The more faith
shines in its splendor, the more radiant will be the
light it reflects upon itself. He who really believes
with a true and living faith will also know that he believes, and will be ready to affirm that he believes,
even though he should at times be prompted to add
the prayer, "help thou mine unbelief." This does not
mean, however, that he will always be clearly aware
of the security, the safety, and the joy that is involved in this assurance.

c. *The Assurance That Is Not Involved in Faith*

But though there is an assurance that is of the
essence of faith, it cannot be said that all assurance
of salvation is necessarily involved in faith. Faith
terminates on the promises of God and in the last
analysis on Jesus Christ as the Saviour of sinners.

It says: God promises to pardon the penitent sinner, to adopt him as his son, and to make him an heir of everlasting life; I embrace those promises, I appropriate them and rest on them for time and eternity. This is an assurance that is based directly on what is revealed in the Word of God. But now the believer can make his own faith or his spiritual condition in general the object of his contemplation or reflection, in order to determine the genuineness of his faith, the soundness of his spiritual state, the validity of his birthright, and the unimpeachable character of his claim to the inheritance of the saints. These things are not revealed in the word of God, and therefore cannot be the proper objects of faith. Neither can the assurance respecting them, which is obtained by reflection, be considered as an assurance that is of the essence of faith.

They who deny that assurance is necessarily involved in faith, and yet hold that believers can obtain the full assurance of salvation, generally claim that this certitude can only result from a logical conclusion from what is technically called "the syllogism of faith," of which the first premise is furnished by Scripture and the second by the regenerated consciousness. The Bible says that whosoever truly believeth is saved; and the Christian confesses that he is conscious of believing with a saving faith, and then draws the conclusion that he is therefore saved. While they who maintain that there is an assurance that is of the essence of faith, are all agreed that this method of seeking assurance is also both Scriptural

and Reformed, they do not all place the same estimate on it. Some consider it to be of secondary
importance, while others regard it as the only way in
which the *full* assurance of faith can be obtained.

It is a method that is recognized by our Confessional Standards. The Heidelberg Catechism asks:
"Since, then, we are redeemed from our misery by
grace through Christ, without any merit of ours, why
must we do good works?" And the answer is in part:
". . . that we ourselves may be assured of our faith
by the fruits thereof." And the Canons of Dort,
after asserting that the assurance of salvation springs
from faith in God's promises, and from the testimony
of the Holy Spirit, also adds: ". . . and, lastly,
from a serious and holy desire to preserve a good
conscience and to perform good works." This is also
in harmony with the assertion of the Westminster
Confession that the assurance of faith is founded on
the promises of God, and on "the inward evidence
of those graces unto which these promises are made."
This method of seeking assurance is not merely Reformed, but also thoroughly Scriptural. The prin-
ciple of it is expressed by Jesus, when he says in
warning against false prophets: "By their fruits ye
shall know them. Do men gather grapes of thorns,
or figs of thistles? Even so every good tree bringeth
forth good fruit; but the corrupt tree bringeth forth
evil fruit." Matt. 7:16, 17. John urged his readers
to love the brethren with an unfeigned love, and declares: "Hereby shall we know that we are of the
truth, and shall assure our heart before him." I

John 3:18, 19. That this method is not quite as simple as it may seem, nor its results as conclusive as might be desirable, will appear in the next chapter. In this connection it is only necessary to call attention to the fact that the assurance so obtained is not of the essence of faith. Neither can we properly consider it as a fruit of the reflex action of faith, though it is often so called. It does not result from an operation of faith at all, but is simply a rational deduction from data supplied by Scripture and by the Christian consciousness.

IV

THE FOUNDATION OF THE ASSURANCE OF FAITH

a. *The Promises of God*

IT WAS one of the great mistakes of the Pietism of the seventeenth and eighteenth centuries that, in seeking the assurance of faith, or of salvation, it divorced itself too much from the Word of God. The basis of assurance was sought, not in the objective promises of the Gospel, but in the subjective experiences of believers. The knowledge of the experiences that were made the touch-stone of faith, was not gathered from the Word of God, but was obtained by an inductive study of the subjective states and affections of believers. In many cases these were not even put to the test of Scripture, so that the true was not always distinguished from the counterfeit. Moreover, there were unwarranted generalizations. Individual experiences and experiences of a very dubious character were often made normative, were set forth as the necessary marks of true faith. The result was that they who were concerned about the welfare of their soul turned attention to themselves rather than to the Word of God, and spent their life in morbid introspection. It is no wonder that this method did not promote the assurance of faith that fills the heart with heavenly joy, but rather en-

gendered doubt and uncertainty and caused the soul
to grope about in a labyrinth of anxious questionings, without an Ariadne-thread to lead it out. This
method of seeking assurance by looking within rather
than by looking without, to Jesus Christ as He is
presented in Scripture, and by making the experiences of others, especially of those who are regarded
as "oaks of righteousness" normative, has not yet
been abandoned entirely in our own circles. Yet it is
a most disappointing one. Archibald Alexander in
his *Thoughts on Religious Experience* quotes the
narrative of a certain R—— C——, who makes the
following pertinent statement: "I had spent much
time in reading accounts of Christian experience, and
those which lay down the marks and evidences of
true religion, such as Owen on *Spiritual-Mindedness,*
Edwards on *The Affections,* Guthrie's *Trial of a
Saving Interest in Christ,* Newton's *Letters,* Pike
and Hayward's *Cases of Conscience,* etc. I also con-
versed much with old and experienced Christians,
as well as with those of my own age. But all these
having, as it seemed to me, very little facilitated my
progress, and the evils of my heart seeming rather to
increase, I hastily resolved to lay aside all books except the Bible, and to devote my whole time to prayer
and reading until I experienced a favourable change."
The sequel shows that he did not make that trial in
vain; by the study of God's Word and prayer he was
led into light.

The experience of R—— C—— points the way. If
we would have the assurance of faith, the first great

requisite is that we make a diligent study of the Bible, and more particularly of the glorious promises of forgiveness and salvation. After all it is only in the Word of God and in the living Christ, as He is mirrored in the Word, that we find the objective basis for the assurance of grace and perseverance to the end. The free promises of God are the foundation of our faith, and it is only on the strength of these that we place our trust in Christ as our Saviour. These promises are absolutely reliable and have their confirmation in Jesus Christ. "For how many soever be the promises of God, in him is the yea; wherefore also through him is the Amen, unto the glory of God through us." II Cor. 1:20. Desiring to give the heirs of salvation full assurance in this respect, God even confirmed his promise by an oath, "that by two immutable things, in which it is impossible for God to lie, we may have a strong encouragement, who have fled for refuge to lay hold of the hope set before us." Heb. 6:18. A real conviction of the truth of the promises inspires trust, and trust confidence, and these, in turn, are the sure foundation of a living hope. The promises are not only sure, but also unconditional, i.e. they are not conditioned by any work of man. This is a very essential element in connection with the assurance of salvation. If they were not entirely gratuitous, they would throw us back upon our own works and thereby make assurance for the future impossible. Calvin says: "Therefore, if we would not have faith to waver and tremble, we must support it with the promise of salvation, which is offered by the Lord spontaneously and freely, from a regard to our misery, rather than our worth." Faith has no firm footing until it rests in the mercy of God. Moreover, the promises of God are all-comprehensive. They make provision for our natural life and for our spiritual needs; they hold out prospects of strength for the weary and of joy for the afflicted; they give the assurance of sufficient grace for the present, of perseverance to the end, and of future blessedness.

But promises do not necessarily constitute a sure foundation for faith and trust and hope. Experience teaches us that many promises fail. Men are often very liberal with their promises, but soon forget about them, or simply ignore them, or find that they have promised more than they can accomplish. And doubly unfortunate are they who accept such promises in good faith, who trust to their fulfilment, and who pin their hopes on them for the future. It is quite evident that the real value of promises as a foundation on which to build depends on the reliability, the faithfulness, and the power of their author. And it is exactly when believers consider the Author of the promises on which they build the house of their hope, and then only, that they are in a position to evaluate them aright and recognize in them a foundation firm and sure. In their perplexity they may occasionally ask, "Hath God forgotten to be gracious?" Yet they may rest assured that He will never forget his people (Isa. 44:21), nor be unmindful of his covenant (Jer. 50:5). He cannot forget

the promises made to his people. "Can a woman
forget her sucking child, that she should not have
compassion on the son of her womb? yea, these may
forget, yet will not I forget thee." Isa. 49:15. Believers may and often do become unfaithful and
ignore their covenant responsibilities, but in spite of
the perversity of his children, God remains faithful
to his covenant. The Bible is full of assurances respecting the faithfulness of God. We find a touch-
ing expression of it in the eighty-ninth psalm, verses
28-34:

"My lovingkindness will I keep him forevermore,
    And my covenant shall stand fast with him.
His seed also will I make to endure for ever,
    And his throne as the days of heaven.
If his children forsake my law,
    And walk not in mine ordinances;
If they break my statutes,
    And keep not my commandments;
Then will I visit their transgression with the rod,
    And their iniquity with stripes.
But my lovingkindness will I not utterly take from
        him,
    Nor suffer my faithfulness to fail.
My covenant will I not break,
    Nor alter the thing that is gone out of my lips."

It is hardly possible to find a stronger statement
of the faithfulness of our covenant God than is found
in Isa. 54:10, "For the mountains may depart, and
the hills be removed; but my lovingkindness shall
not depart from thee, neither shall my covenant of
peace be removed, saith Jehovah, that hath mercy on

thee." But even the faithfulness of God would not be an absolute guarantee for the fulfilment of his promises, were there any power in heaven or on earth that could thwart his gracious purposes. But our covenant God is the Almighty Creator of heaven and earth, the Ruler of the universe, who holds all things in the hollow of his hand, and has absolute control of all powers and principalities. In connection with the incredulous laughter of Sarah the Lord said: "Is anything too hard for Jehovah?" The expected answer to this question is an absolute negative. Of Abraham we are told that he believed against hope. Though the fulfilment of the promise which he had received seemed to be a physical impossibility, he wavered not through unbelief, but was fully assured that what God had promised He was able also to perform. A similar faith finds expression in the words of Paul: . . . "for I know Him whom I have believed, and I am persuaded that He is able to guard that which I have committed unto Him against that day." II Tim. 1:12.

Now the believer's trust in God and in Jesus Christ for the blessings of grace and the joys of salvation is based on the promises of their covenant God. These constitute the only objective foundation on which he can build. And the measure in which he trusts in Christ and thus appropriates the promises of the Gospel will, if all other things are equal, also determine the strength or weakness of the feeling of security that fills the heart, and the degree of the consciousness that his sins are forgiven, and that he

is an heir of everlasting life. Isaiah says: "They
that wait for Jehovah (i.e. who trust in Him and are
confident that He will fulfill his promises) shall renew
their strength; they shall mount up with wings as
eagles; they shall run and not be weary; they shall
walk and not faint." 40:31. Mindful of the comfort-
ing significance of the statutes of the Lord, which are
regarded as including his promises, the psalmist
sings: "Thy statutes have been my songs in the
house of my pilgrimage." Ps. 119:54. Well may
believers utter their joy in the words of the well-
known hymn:

> "How firm a foundation, ye saints of the Lord,
> Is laid for your faith in his excellent Word!
> What more can he say than to you He hath said,
> To you who for refuge to Jesus have fled?

> "Fear not, I am with thee; oh, be not dismayed!
> For I am thy God; I will still give thee aid;
> I'll strengthen thee, help thee, and cause thee to stand,
> Upheld by my righteous omnipotent hand.

> "When through the deep waters I call thee to go,
> The rivers of sorrow shall not overflow;
> For I will be with thee thy troubles to bless,
> And sanctify to thee thy deepest distress.

> "When through fiery trials thy pathway shall lie,
> My grace all sufficient shall be thy supply;
> The flame shall not harm thee; I only design
> The dross to consume, and thy gold to refine.

> "The soul that on Jesus hath leaned for repose
> I will not, I will not desert to his foes;
> That soul, though all hell should endeavor to shake,
> I'll never, no never, no never forsake."

b. *The Witness of the Holy Spirit*

But the promises of God, no matter how beautiful and reliable, are not in and by themselves sufficient to awaken faith in the heart of the sinner. They are not seen in their beauty and strength until the eye of faith is opened by the operation of the Holy Spirit. And after faith has been wrought in the heart, it is ever dependent on the Spirit for its progressive growth and its increasing maturity. It is through the illuminating influence of the Holy Spirit that the light gradually dawns on the Gospel promises, increases in strength, and finally reaches its mid-day height. Again, the first faltering steps that give evidence of trust in Christ, the increasing confidence based on the promises of the Gospel, and the final complete self-surrender to Christ,—they are all fruits of the Spirit. In view of all this it is but natural that we should have alongside of the objective ground of assurance in the promises of God, also a subjective ground in the witness of the Holy Spirit. Both are clearly recognized in the Canons of Dort: "This assurance, however, is not produced by any peculiar revelation contrary to, or independent of the Word of God, but springs from faith in God's promises, which He has most abundantly revealed in his Word for our comfort; from the testimony of the Holy Spirit, witnessing with our spirit, that we are children and heirs of God (Rom. 8:16) ; and, lastly, from a serious and holy desire to preserve a good conscience, and to perform good works.

There is good Scriptural evidence for such a witnessing of the Holy Spirit. The most famous passage containing this truth, is Rom. 8: 15-17, "For ye received not the spirit of bondage again to fear; but ye received the spirit of adoption, whereby we cry, Abba, Father. The Spirit himself beareth witness with our spirit, that we are children of God; and if children, then heirs, heirs of God, and joint-heirs with Christ." A similar note is sounded, though not with the same fulness, in Gal. 4:6, "And because ye are sons, God sent forth the Spirit of his Son into our hearts, crying, Abba, Father." Again, we hear an echo of the same truth in a slightly different form in I Cor. 2:12, "But we received, not the spirit of the world, but the spirit which is from God; that we might know the things that were freely given us of God." The Holy Spirit is clearly set before us in Scripture as a witness, witnessing particularly to Christ and his saving work. He witnesses to the objective truth revealed in Christ, both in and through the disciples, John 15:26; 16; 13-15; Acts 5:32; I John 5:7, 9, 10; and also to the life of Christ in the hearts of believers, that expresses itself in a holy conversation.

Though the fact of the Spirit's witnessing to the sonship of believers is well established by Scripture, there is considerable difference of opinion as to the manner in which He gives his testimony. Our Confessional Standards simply speak of the "testimony of the Holy Spirit, witnessing with our spirit, that we are children and heirs of God." This statement clearly proceeds on the assumption, based on Rom. 8:16, that there is a joint testimony of the spirit of believers and of the Holy Spirit, but does not indicate the precise nature of this testimony. Wesley and the Wesleyan Methodists conceive of the witness of the Holy Spirit as being of the nature of an immediate and overpowering impression upon the soul, almost if not quite a special revelation, at the time of the believer's justification, respecting his spiritual state. Says Wesley: "By the testimony of the Spirit, I mean an inward impression on the soul, whereby the Spirit of God immediately and directly witnesses to my spirit that I am a child of God, that Jesus Christ hath loved me and given himself for me, that all my sins are blotted out, and I, even I, am reconciled to God." He distinguishes sharply between the witness of the Holy Spirit and that of the spirit of believers, and regards the latter as an inferential judgment, based on a comparison of the believer's experience with the Scriptural delineation of the Christian life. It is really the result of reflection on the Christian graces which the believer discovers in his own soul.

Reformed theologians generally have a somewhat different conception of the testimony of the Holy Spirit, added to that of our own spirit. While some are inclined to think that Paul in Rom. 8:15, 16 speaks of but a single witness, that of the Holy Spirit, the majority are of the opinion that he has two witnesses in mind, the witness of the believing spirit and that of the Spirit of God. There can be little doubt that the apostle refers to a double testimony. At the same time it is perfectly clear that he conceives of the two as most intimately related, the one as grounded in the other. This is evident from the fact that, according to Rom. 8:15, believers cry "in the Spirit," Abba, Father; and that Gal. 4:6 represents this cry as that of the Spirit himself. It may be said that the Spirit of God testifies through our spirit, but also to our spirit.

Even in Reformed circles the testimony of the human spirit is often represented as being exclusively the product of a reflective process, and not at all the result of a spontaneous conviction which issues, without any consciousness of argumentative procedure, from living spiritual affections. And yet it would seem that Paul has in mind such an instinctive witnessing, when he says that we cry in the Spirit, Abba, Father. Certainly a man's judgment, on reviewing himself and finding that he has the fruits of the Spirit, is a witness of his own spirit that he is a child of God. "But," says Sheldon, "there is a swifter and intenser witness than this. The mother whose heart is actually bound up in her child does not need, in order to convince herself that she has parental love, to reflect upon an approved catalogue of the fruits of parental love. The outgoing of her heart to her offspring is an immediate experience of parental love, an original knowledge which reflection may ratify, but to whose vivacity and certainty it can add little or nothing. So spiritual emotions and affections in the heart,—the feeling of trust, the

blended reverence and confidence, the joyful compla-
cency which accompanies the thought of God, the
thirst for divine fellowship, and the sense of that
fellowship,—irradiate one's relation to God before
time is taken for any formal induction." And it is
just this immediate consciousness of love to God, of
trust and confidence in him, of reverence and childlike fear, of longings for God and satisfaction in his
blessed communion, and of joy in obedient service,
that prompts the spontaneous cry, arising from the
depths of the soul, "Abba, Father." It is a human
cry, but a cry of divine origin, born of the Spirit
of God.

But the believer, knowing the deceitfulness of his
own heart, and conscious of his inability to understand, to fathom, and to evaluate the deep things of
God, may be inclined to doubt his own testimony, especially in seasons of spiritual darkness and when
satan sows the seeds of distrust in the heart. Therefore the apostle points to the fact that there is another
and more fundamental testimony than that of the
human consciousness; a testimony of one who knows,
a testimony that is absolutely reliable, a testimony
that can never be invalidated. It is the testimony of
the Holy Spirit, who knows the deep things of God,
who is absolutely infallible in his judgment, and who
will maintain his estimate of believers in spite of all
adversaries. "The spirit himself beareth witness
with (or, to) our spirit, that we are children of God."
If the believer confidently addresses God as his Father
in heaven, God recognizes the believer as his child.

This testimony of the Holy Spirit should not be conceived of as a communication, conveyed to the believer by a secret voice, and giving him the assurance that he is a child of God; nor as a specific operation of the Holy Spirit on the mind, by which he directs attention to a passage of Scripture containing that assurance. Neither should it be regarded as a testimony that is given once for all at the moment of conversion, to which the believer can confidently appeal ever after, no matter whether he be yielding the fruits of the Spirit, or be following the lusts of the flesh. The Spirit of God testifies continually by his indwelling in the hearts of those that fear the Lord, and by all those gracious operations in the renewal of man that are so manifestly divine. He opens the eye of faith to the beauty and glory of the promises of God, illumines the mind so that their spiritual import is understood, and fills the heart with a sense of their appropriateness for lost sinners. He discloses to the spiritual eye the gracious character of the Saviour, causes the sinner to flee to him for refuge and to seek shelter in the shadow of his wings, and leads the soul to a trustful repose, safe in the arms of Jesus. He speaks in all the movements of the new life: in the love of God that is shed abroad in our hearts, in the filial spirit, the spirit of love and reverence and obedience, in his intercessions in the inner man with groanings that cannot be uttered, in the manifold experiences of comfort in suffering, strength in weakness, victory in seasons of temptation, and perseverence under the trials of faith.

These are all works of the Holy Spirit. In so far as they are in us and abound, they bear witness to the reality of our reconciliation with God, and in the very voice of the Spirit give us the assurance that our sins are forgiven and that we are children of God. These vital spiritual affections shine with their own light, and thus constitute the testimony of the Holy Spirit that carries conviction to the soul. The more the life of faith develops, the greater our progress in the way of sanctification, the clearer will the voice of the spirit ring out, dispelling all doubts and filling the heart with joy and peace.

We meet with a closely related idea, where Paul speaks of the Holy Spirit as a seal with which believers are sealed, and as an earnest of their inheritance. This twofold significance of the Spirit finds expression in a single passage, Eph. 1:13, 14 . . . "in whom, having also believed, ye were sealed with the Holy Spirit of promise, which is an earnest of our inheritance, unto the redemption of God's own possession, unto the praise of his glory." Now a seal is used for various purposes: (1) to authenticate or mark as true and genuine; (2) to mark as one's property; and (3) to insure security or safety. The sealing of believers has this threefold significance. Being in possession of the Holy Spirit, they have the witness within themselves that they are true children of God, I John 5:10; Rom. 5:5; 8:16. By the seal of the Spirit that is impressed upon them they are also marked as belonging to God, so that others readily recognize them as children of God. Moreover, the fact that they are said to be sealed unto the day of redemption, Eph. 4:30, clearly indicates that the sealing of God secures their safety, that they are thereby rendered sure of their final salvation. The Spirit is even the earnest of their inheritance. In him believers possess the first fruits of the full harvest of salvation that will be reaped in the great day of the coming of Jesus Christ.

c. *The Testimony of the Christian Graces*

Finally, Reformed Confessional Standards also clearly indicate that assurance is based in part on the so-called syllogism of faith, in which the believer consciously and deliberately compares the graces that adorn his life and his general conduct, with the biblical description of the virtues and the godly conversation of those who are born of the Spirit, and on their relative correspondence bases the conclusion that he is indeed a child of God. The Bible says: "Blessed are the poor in spirit, . . . blessed are they that mourn, ... blessed are the meek, ... blessed are they that hunger and thirst after righteousness," etc. And the believer who is purposely in quest of assurance examines his heart and life to discover, whether he is poor in spirit and truly humble, and whether he mourns on account of his sin and really hungers and thirsts after righteousness. His self-examination determines the conclusion to which he comes. If he finds that these graces do really and

truly adorn his life, he will naturally infer from this
that he belongs to the number of those whom Jesus
pronounces blessed.

It is quite evident that in this logical deduction we
are operating with premises derived from the two
grounds of assurance to which attention was called
in the preceding, viz. the promises of God in his
Word and the testimony of the Holy Spirit in the
hearts and lives of believers. When the Holy Spirit
originates, strengthens, and increases faith in God's
children so that they not only begin but also continue
to appropriate the promises of God, this will at once
carry with it a certain measure of assurance. It may
be that this instinctive and immediate assurance will
be but vaguely felt at first; but it will naturally rise
to the level of a conscious certitude in the measure in
which faith increases and becomes abundant in spiritual fruits, and often rises to that height without any
conscious reflection on the grounds, the nature and
the operations of faith. Many Christians who enjoy
the assurance of faith are not able to give an intelligent explanation of it, and are at a loss what to say
when they are asked for the grounds of their assurance, or for proof of the genuineness of their faith.
They may be able only to repeat the words of the
man whom Jesus cured of his blindness: "One thing
I know, that, whereas I was blind, now I see." Their
lack of clear knowledge on this point, however, may
cause them to reflect on the nature and grounds of
their faith, and on the evidences of the life of the
spirit that is born within their hearts. And then

they are invariably led to base their assurance consciously and deliberately on the objective promises of God in connection with the subjective fruits of the Spirit.

This method of seeking assurance is perfectly Scriptural. While Paul emphasizes the significance of the inner witness of the spirit in connection with the assurance of faith, John lays the chief stress on the ethical tests of faith and thus illustrates the method now under consideration. "We know," says he, "that we have passed out of death into life, because we love the brethren." I John 3:14. Referring to that same test of love to the brethren, a love in deed and truth, he continues in the 19th verse of the same chapter: "Hereby we shall know that we are of the truth, and shall assure our heart before him." Again, he sounds the language of assurance in the words: "We know that we have come to a knowledge of him, if we keep his commandments," 2:3; and, "Whoso keepeth his word, in him verily hath the love of God been perfected. Hereby we know that we are in him: he that saith he abideth in him ought himself also to walk even as he walked," 2:5, 6. We may find the same line of thought indicated in II Pet. 1:5-10, where the apostle exhorts his readers to assure themselves of their calling and election by adding to faith virtue, to virtue knowledge, to knowledge temperance, to temperance patience, to patience godliness, to godliness brotherly love, and to brotherly love, love to all.

But it is quite possible to expect too much of this

method of comparison. It seems to be a very easy
matter, but in reality it is extremely difficult. Dis-
appointment may follow the attempt to gain assurance by contemplating the fruits of faith. There are
several reasons for this. The inner life of man, and
especially the religious side of it, is very complicated
and therefore constitutes a difficult field to explore.
Moreover, in view of the deceitfulness of man's
heart, it is not easy to maintain strict impartiality,
seeing that he who collects the evidence and passes
judgment on it, is also the interested party. By nature man is not inclined to see himself just as he is,
in all his sinfulness and corruption; and even in the
regenerated man it requires a large measure of grace
to overcome this natural aversion. Then, too, a
faithful self-inspection usually reveals so much that
is defective, that the first result is apt to be discour-
agement rather than the glad assurance of hope.
Again, in testing the genuineness of his faith by good
works as the fruit of faith, a person may find that he
is after all merely reasoning in a circle. The question naturally arises, What are good works? And
the Heidelberg Catechism answers: "Those only
which are done from true faith, according to the law
of God, for his glory." He who would know whether
his faith is genuine, must investigate, whether
it bears real spiritual fruit; and in order to determine whether the fruit is genuine, he must consider
whether it springs from a true and living faith. And
finally, it should be borne in mind that, while genuine fruits of righteousness do indeed testify to the

presence of a living faith, the fact that these fruits have not yet made their appearance does not prove the absence of true faith. How extremely difficult it is to distinguish a Christian from a non-Christian by their respective fruits is clearly apparent from the attempts of some eighteenth century theologians to discriminate between the believer at his worst and the unbeliever at his best. In order to know men by their fruits, the real character of these fruits must be clearly apparent.

It would seem to be a mistake, therefore, to make a comparison of the graces that adorn the Christian's life and the requirements of God, together with the self-inspection which it involves, the only or even the chief ground of his assurance. It can only serve to confirm a conviction that is already more or less present in the mind, and in many cases adds little or nothing to the assurance of faith. Where faith is weak and does not reveal its vitality in the development of Christian graces and in the production of good works, there is no subjective basis for the comparison, and therefore no ground for the certitude of faith. And where faith is strong and vital and abounds in spiritual fruits, it carries an immediate assurance with it, which a deliberate comparison would not be able to make more sure, though it might render it more intelligible. Whatever assurance may be attained in this way, can only result from a true spiritual insight into the promises of God; from a self-examination that is performed with candid honesty, with great thoroughness, in a prayerful frame of mind, and above all under the illuminating influence of the Holy Spirit; and from a conclusion that is based on a correct interpretation of the promises of God, and of such Christian graces as are clearly and unmistakably recognized as fruits of the Spirit.

Some object to this method of seeking assurance altogether. They claim that it directs believers to seek the ground of assurance within themselves, and thus encourages them to build on a self-righteous foundation. But this is clearly a mistake. Believers are not taught to regard their good works as the meritorious cause of their salvation, but only as the divinely wrought evidences of a faith that is itself a gift of God. Their conclusion is based exactly on the assumption that the qualities and works which they discover in their life, could never have been wrought by themselves, but can only be regarded as the products of sovereign grace.

V

THE ABSENCE AND CULTIVATION OF ASSURANCE

a. *The Absence of Assurance*

"THIS infallible assurance," says the Westminster Confession, "doth not so belong to the essence of faith, but that a true believer may wait long, and conflict with many difficulties before he be partaker of it." These words embody the objection that is often raised to the position that assurance is of the essence of faith. The argument is that, if it were, believers would be sure of being in a state of grace, and consequently also of their future salvation, from the very moment of their accepting Jesus Christ as their Saviour. But both Scripture and experience teach that in reality the situation is quite different. The Bible contains examples of saints that are lost in a maze of perplexities and are struggling with doubt and uncertainty; exhorts believers to examine themselves as to whether they are in the faith; and urges them to strive for the full assurance of faith and hope. Moreover, experience teaches us that there are many serious-minded people, who lead a truly Christian life and thus give evidence of sharing the life of the Spirit, and nevertheless grope about in uncertainty and hesitate to affirm that they are children of God and heirs of eternal life. Sometimes even those who had apparently obtained a sure footing in the promises of God, who experienced a temporary assurance, and rejoiced for a season in the hope of salvation, are cast back upon the waves of doubt and find reason to cry out:

"But ah! too soon my fears return,
And dark mistrust disturbs anew;
What smothered fires within yet burn!
My days of peace, alas, how few!
These heart-throes,—shall they ne'er be past?
These strifes,—shall they forever last?

It would seem to follow, therefore, that faith does not always carry assurance with it, that believers may remain in doubt for a long time and will perhaps never in this life enter into the light of Christian certitude.

We should bear in mind, however, that they who assert that assurance belongs to the essence of faith, generally want it clearly understood that this does not imply that all believers at once, or at least after a very short time, enjoy the full assurance of salvation; nor that, after this has been obtained, it may not be shaken and undiminished and even for a time appear completely lost in doubt and perplexity. Calvin fully admits and enlarges on this possibility. And the Synod of Dort, no less than the Westminster divines, testifies to the fact that believers in this life have to struggle with various carnal doubts, and are not always sensible of the full assurance of faith and of the certainty of persevering. No other note is sounded by the Marrow-men of Scotland, who were accused of teaching and did actually teach that assurance is of the essence of faith. There are two extremes that should be avoided: on the one hand the position that it is possible to have a true living faith without any degree of subjective assurance; and on the other hand the standpoint of Jean de Labadie that no one is in a state of grace who does not have absolute assurance. Though there is a subjective certitude that is of the essence of faith, it is quite possible that a true believer will, for a considerable time, lack the consciousness of this blessed assurance.

This will hardly be fully understood without bearing several distinctions in mind. In the first place it is necessary to remember that assurance is not always of the same kind. We should distinguish between the assurance that is implicit in faith and that which becomes explicit in consciousness. The former may be merely a general sense of security, of which the believer does not even give himself a clear account, and that does not yet give him courage to say that his sins are forgiven, or that he is a child of God and an heir of eternal life. At the same time it is of the utmost importance, because it is the germ of all further assurance. Quite different from this assurance that is involved even in the first act of faith, is the certitude that results from the continued and ever increasing activity of faith, that gradually rises into clear consciousness and is often called "the full assurance of faith." It consists in the blessed

certainty of the believer that he is incorporated into
Jesus Christ, that his sins are pardoned, and that he
is already in possession of a salvation that will issue
in eternal glory. Though he who has accepted Christ
by faith always has a certain sense of security in believing, however vague it may be, he may live for a
long time without this full assurance of faith, an
assurance that is firm even in the most adverse
circumstances, and that enables its possessor to hope
against hope.

It is already apparent from the preceding that we
cannot make the distinction between different kinds
of assurance without distinguishing between faith in
its initial stages and faith in its more developed form.
Just as a new-born babe is at once perfect in parts,
containing all that is necessary unto the making of
a man, so true faith is at once perfect in parts but
not yet in degree. Scripture clearly teaches us that
there are different degrees in faith. Christians are
exhorted to exercise the gifts imparted to them "according to the proportion" (or, "measure") of their
faith (Rom. 12:6). There are examples of a weak
and of a strong, of a little and of a great faith. The
disciples pray, "Increase our faith" (Luke 17:5),
and Paul trusts that, as their "faith groweth," the
Corinthians will have a more favorable opinion of
him (II Cor. 10:15). He gives thanks to God because the faith of the Thessalonians "groweth ex-
ceedingly" (II Thess. 1:3). And the writer of Hebrews speaks of "babes" and "full-grown men,"
Heb. 5:13, 14. Now a little faith naturally carries

with it but a small measure of assurance, while an abundant faith is marked by a certitude that fills the heart with a joyous hope. Experience teaches us that believers, as a rule, gradually grow into the full assurance of faith, though in cases in which they are brought to Christ by a sudden and tremendous change, they may experience a great measure of assurance at once.

Another distinction that should be borne in mind, is that between faith as it is in itself and faith as it is exercised by different believers and in various circumstances of life. While faith in itself always includes a measure of assurance, it is possible to exercise faith in such a way that this element is not properly developed. There are some believers who stress the element of knowledge in faith at the expense of that of the trustful repose that is also essential to a well balanced faith. Some find it comparatively easy to lose sight of themselves and their works and to look only to Christ, while others are much given to introspection and habitually look in a direction in which no assurance can be found. There are those who are deeply conscious of the fact that their good works are in no sense meritorious, and who contemplate them exclusively as the fruits of faith; but there are also such as, perhaps unconsciously, proceed on the assumption that their salvation depends, at least in part, on their good works, and thus render assurance impossible. Again, there are Christians that have their eyes fixed primarily on the threatenings contained in the Word of God, while others preferably dwell on the glorious promises of salvation in Jesus Christ. These differences are bound to result in different degrees of assurance. There may be various circumstances that rob the believer of the desired certitude of faith. A sense of great unworthiness may sometimes cause him to hesitate in the appropriation of the Gospel promises. Spiritual apathy may shroud his soul in a darkness that renders the joy of salvation impossible. Severe trials may fill his heart with doubts as to the goodness, the love, and the mercy of his God. And the direct assaults of satan may rob him of the peace of God that passes all understanding.

It is quite possible therefore that a believer may go without the full assurance of faith for a long time. It is also possible for him to lose it again after he has possessed it for some time. The Bible testifies to this in recording some of the experiences of the saints. The poet of the forty-second psalm was evidently a man of faith; yet he found occasion to ask: "Why art thou cast down, O, my Soul? And why are thou disquieted within me?" David, the man after God's own heart, even said in his haste: "I am cut off from before thine eyes " Ps. 31:22. Asaph debated within his soul respecting the mercy and faithfulness of God: "Will the Lord cast off forever? And will He be favorable no more? Is His lovingkindness clean gone forever? Doth his promise fail for evermore? Hath God forgotten to be gracious? Hath He in anger shut up his tender mercies?" Ps. 77:7-9. It is evident, however, from the connection in which these expressions of disquietude, perplexity, and doubt occur, that these saints even in their distress did not cease to trust their God, were not entirely devoid of a feeling of security, and through their struggles again rose to the height of confident assurance.

The opposite of assurance is doubt, and the lack of assurance means the presence of doubt. It is necessary to remember, however, that doubt is not always of the same kind. There may be doubts respecting the objective truths of the Gospel, but also doubts respecting one's spiritual state. The former are always signs of unbelief, the latter, however deplorable and even culpable they may be, do not necessarily spring from unbelief. They may be merely the result of ignorance. There are four words in the New Testament that point to the doubt of the distracted mind, a doubt that reveals itself in wavering from faith, and that results in anxious questionings. This doubt presupposes the presence of faith, for only those who have faith can waver or be distracted from it. "But the faith to which it witnesses," says Dr. Warfield, "is equally necessarily an incomplete and imperfect faith; only an imperfect faith can waver or be distracted from its firm assurance." Such were the doubts of those whom the Saviour describes as having "little faith." Cf: also Luke 24:38; Rom. 14:1. But there is also a term that points, not merely to the weakness, but to the lack of faith. It denotes a critical attitude toward divine things, and where this attitude is found faith is absent. This doubt is not merely the opposite of assurance, but of faith it-self. Cf. Matt. 21:21; Rom. 4:20; 14:23; Jas. 1:6; Jude 22.

b. *The Cultivation of Assurance*

In connection with the fact that believers are often weak in faith and distracted by doubts, and that these doubts may in some cases argue the lack of faith, the Bible urges them to examine themselves closely, and exhorts them to cultivate assurance. It would hardly do to place great emphasis on I Cor. 11:28, for in that passage the apostle does not stress the necessity of examining into the presence or gen-uineness of faith. His main desire is that the Corin-thians shall search their hearts to see, whether they have proper views of the Lord's Supper, and whether they are in a fit frame of mind to celebrate it worth-ily. But the situation is different in II Cor. 13:5, where the apostle says: "Try your own selves, whether ye are in the faith; prove your own selves. Or know ye not as to your own selves, that Jesus Christ is in you? unless indeed ye be reprobate." The exhortation of Peter is entirely in line with this: "Wherefore, brethren, give the more diligence to make your calling and election sure." II Pet. 1:10. This admonition does not proceed on the assumption that there is an element of uncertainty in calling and election, but simply presupposes that they to whom it is directed may be or actually are uncertain in their own minds as to whether they have been called by the Spirit of God and elected unto eternal salvation. The apostle desires that they shall make their calling and election sure for their own consciousness, and also, as far as possible, in the estimation of their fellow-Christians. The Bible certainly does not regard a state of doubt as the normal condition of believers. Their fundamental tone, as recorded in Scriptures, is one of glad assurance. At the same time it is clearly indicated that their faith may be weak, that they may be distracted by doubts, may be wandering about in a maze of uncertainty, and may be groping in spiritual darkness. But this is not presented as their normal condition. It is rather made to appear as subnormal or even abnormal; and the believer is exhorted to cultivate assurance.

An important question emerges at this point. How should the Christian cultivate the assurance of salvation? What method should he employ in his endeavor to obtain Christian certitude? If what was said in the preceding is not entirely beside the mark, then the best way to strive for the assurance of salvation is simply the diligent cultivation of an ever increasing life of faith. And this can best be done by the ordinary means which God has placed at our disposal, i. e., by a diligent study of the Word of God, more particularly of the blessed promises that are yea and amen in Jesus Christ; by a constant and earnest prayer for the quickening influences of the Holy Spirit, the Spirit of adoption; by faithful attendance to the means of grace, both the Word and the sacraments, through which the Holy Spirit strengthens the good work which He has begun in the hearts of believers; and by the careful cultivation of those Christian graces that are the natural fruits of a living faith, for a slothful Christian cannot expect to enjoy the blessed assurance of salvation. The more our faith grows, the greater will be our assurance. The Christians of the Hebrews, who were abundant in their work of love, in ministering to the saints, are exhorted to show the same diligence unto the full assurance of hope even to the end, that they may be imitators of them who *through faith* and patience inherit the promises, Heb. 6:11, 12. And Peter exhorts his readers to make their calling and election sure by cultivating a Christian disposition, by adding to their faith (as the root) "virtue, and to virtue knowledge, and to knowledge temperance, and to temperance patience, and to patience godliness, and to godliness brotherly love, and to brotherly love, love to all," II Pet. 1:5-7, 10.

But it is well to remember that there is also an assurance that is the fruit of reflection. When we seek to give ourselves an intelligent account of our Christian certitude, we resort to analysis and comparison, and thus endeavor, as far as possible, to obtain a rational insight into our assurance. Such an attempt is often prompted by the disturbing questions, whether we really have faith, and whether the faith we claim is a real and living faith. Such questions ordinarily do not arise, when faith is strong and active and abundant in good works, but when it is weak and lethargic and does not abound in the fruits of the Spirit. In seeking assurance, the believer then searches, not the lives of other Christians, but the Scriptures for the marks and signs of true faith, and finds that these consist, among others, in a childlike spirit, confidence in God and in Jesus Christ, love to God and a holy desire to do his will, sorrow on account of sin and a longing for holiness, hatred of sin and of the forces of evil, and an earnest endeavor to battle against the enemies of the Kingdom of God. With these in mind he examines himself to discover, whether they are present in his life at least in some degree. The clearer these Christian graces shine forth and the more abundant they are, the greater will be the measure of assurance which they engender. He who finds within himself the fruit of the Spirit, such as "love, joy, peace, longsuffering, kindness, goodness, faithfulness, meekness, self-control" (Gal. 5:22), may be sure that the Spirit of God is operative in his heart; and because this is the Spirit of adoption, he may rest assured that he is a child of God.

VI

THE GLORY OF ASSURANCE

THE assurance of salvation is one of the most precious gifts of God, and one that ought to be highly appreciated by all believers. It is true, Roman Catholics and Arminians do not regard it as a desirable attainment, for in their estimation it is detrimental to true holiness and ministers to carnal security and spiritual pride. And even some Reformed Christians chime in with them and sing the praises of doubt. They are inclined to regard the assurance in which others rejoice as a false security, as a pretention of peace when there is no peace, and as a sure sign of self-righteousness and arrogance. They often regard a state of constant doubt, not only as wholesome, but also as a mark of true piety. It is to be feared that they sometimes pretend to doubt, when they do not doubt at all. Their doubt becomes their pride. It would be well for them to reflect for a moment on the fact that in their praise of doubt they join hands with Roman Catholics and Arminians, i. e., with those who are not inclined to seek their salvation entirely without themselves in Jesus Christ, but depend at least in part on their good works. This might open their eyes to the probability that, not those who glory in their assurance, but they themselves are guilty of self-righteousness.

It is highly desirable that the believer should have the assurance of salvation. This may be inferred from the fact that they are exhorted "to show the same diligence to the full assurance of hope to the end" (Heb. 6:11), and to "give diligence to make their calling and election sure" (II Pet. 1:10). In order to avoid misunderstanding, however, it may be well to stress the fact at the outset, that the full assurance of faith is not absolutely essential to the being of a Christian. Boston correctly remarks that "one may go to heaven in a mist, not knowing whither he is going." Our salvation depends on our state and not our knowledge of it.

But if this full assurance is not necessary to the being of a Christian, it is necessary to his well-being. The Christian is in duty bound to lead a life of true gratitude. He must reveal his gratefulness in words of thanksgiving that arise from the heart, in songs of thanksgiving that flow from the lips, and above all in a life of consecrated service. He is redeemed by the blood of the Lamb from the misery of sin, and is therefore prompted to ask:

> "What shall I render to the Lord
> For all his benefits to me?
> How shall my soul by grace restored
> Give worthy thanks, O Lord, to Thee?"

But that question will hardly arise, if he is not certain that he has been redeemed, that his sins are pardoned, and that he has been accepted as a child of

God. He will not feel constrained to give thanks to God for that of which he is not sure that he has received it. He will hardly be in a position to answer with the poet: "I will take the cup of salvation, and call upon the name of the Lord. I will pay my vows unto the Lord, yea, in the presence of all his people."

The Christian's life is intended to be a life of service in the Kingdom of God. He is a vessel of honour, sanctified, meet for the Master's use, prepared unto every good work. And the service that is required of him is arduous and even partakes of the nature of a warfare. The believer is a soldier of Jesus Christ, engaged in earnest battles with the powers of evil. Hence he is urged to put on the whole armour of God, that he may retain his position in the Kingdom of God and frustrate the works of the devil. He needs all the spiritual strength at his disposal, especially the strength that comes from a living and active faith, and from the assurance of salvation. If his gait is halting and uncertain, if his arms are unsteady, if his eye is not clear and true, and if he is lacking in confidence, he will not be able to do his best for the Captain of his salvation. But if he stands in the assurance of faith, he will march to the battle with confidence, will occupy a strong position, will aim with precision, and will fight with the strength that comes from the confident expectation of victory. They whose hearts are always filled with doubts and are constantly engaged in seeking assurance, are like the soldier that spends all his time seeking his armour or in putting it in shape, and meanwhile loses sight of the oncoming forces of the enemy.

The Bible clearly testifies to the fact that God's children must contend with many difficulties and are frequently subject to temptations and trials. Not only do they share in the general sufferings of mankind; they are also called upon to shoulder the cross and to bear the reproach of Jesus Christ. If under such circumstances they have the assurance of faith and are confident of the fact that they are children of God and that He is their loving Father, they will not only have strength to bear the cross, but also grace to rejoice in tribulations. They will stand firm in the conviction that a heavenly Father governs their life and all its circumstances, that the trials and adversities that are sent to them are but parental chastisements that minister to their spiritual welfare, that in all their afflictions they enjoy the support of the everlasting arms which will carry them through, and that the light affliction of the present will issue in an eternal weight of glory. In that conviction they sing with the poet: "Many are the afflictions of the righteous; but Jehovah delivereth him out of them all"; and rejoice with Paul: "For I reckon that the sufferings of the present time are not worthy to be compared with the glory which shall be revealed in us." Without the assurance of faith, however, they will prove weak when the clouds gather, when the darkness thickens, and when the storms of life beat upon their frail vessel. Then distrust sits at the helm, fear fills the heart, anxious questionings arise, and a dissatisfied spirit vents itself in subdued murmurings or in bold outspoken protests. The doubting believer is "like the surge of the sea, driven by the wind and tossed."

Finally, the assurance of faith fills the hearts with the joy of salvation. Surely, of all the children of men none have such abundant reasons to "rejoice and be exceeding glad" as they who have received the Spirit of adoption. They are partakers of the greatest possible honour in that they are children of God, and as children heirs of eternal life. Therefore Paul says: "Rejoice in the Lord always; again I will say, rejoice." Now they who lack the assurance of faith and are given to constant doubts, banish the joy of salvation from their hearts and out of their lives, and often go about as if they were of all men most pitiable. Let the children of God stand upon the heights of assurance and permit the light of heaven to fall upon their earthly life. Then they will go their way rejoicing, and when they reach the last station of the journey, they will serenely face death in the firm conviction that when the house of this tabernacle is broken, they will have a building from God, a house not made with hands, eternal in the heavens. They rejoice in the assurance that the day of their death is but the birthday to a better life. And looking back upon their past life and forward to their eternal home, they join with rapture in the swansong of the apostle: "I have fought the good fight, I have finished the course, I have kept the faith: henceforth there is laid up for me the crown of righteousness, which the Lord, the righteous Judge, shall give me at that day; and not to me only, but to all them that have loved his appearing." II Tim. 4:7, 8.

"Wherefore, brethren, give the more diligence to make your calling and election sure; for if ye do these things ye shall never stumble: for thus shall be richly supplied to you the entrance into the eternal kingdom of our Lord and Saviour Jesus Christ." II Pet. 1:10, 11.

Some Other SGCB Classic Reprints

In addition to *The Assurance of Faith* which you hold in your hand, we are delighted to list several other titles available from Solid Ground Christian Books, many for the first time in a century or more:

A SHEPHERD'S HEART: *Sermons from the Pastoral Ministry of J.W. Alexander*

THEOLOGY ON FIRE: *Sermons from the Heart of J.A. Alexander*

OPENING SCRIPTURE: *A Hermeneutical Manual* by Patrick Fairbairn

THE PASTOR IN THE SICK ROOM by John D. Wells

THE NATIONAL PREACHER: *Revival Sermons from the 2nd Great Awakening*

THE POOR MAN'S NT COMMENTARY by Robert Hawker

THE POOR MAN'S OT COMMENTARY by Robert Hawker

THE POOR MAN'S MORNING & EVENING PORTION by Robert Hawker

FIRST THINGS by Gardiner Spring

BIBLICAL & THEOLOGICAL STUDIES by Princeton Professors of 1912

THE POWER OF GOD UNTO SALVATION by B.B. Warfield

THE LORD OF GLORY by B.B. Warfield

CHRIST ON THE CROSS by John Stevenson

SERMONS TO THE NATURAL MAN by W.G.T. Shedd

SERMONS TO THE SPIRITUAL MAN by W.G.T. Shedd

HOMILETICS & PASTORAL THEOLOGY by W.G.T. Shedd

A PASTOR'S SKETCHES 1 & 2 by B.B. Warfield

CHRIST IN SONG: *Hymns of Immanuel from all ages* by Philip Schaff

THE PREACHER & HIS MODELS by James Stalker

IMAGO CHRISTI by James Stalker

LECTURES ON THE HISTORY OF PREACHING by John A. Broadus

A HISTORY OF PREACHING (2 VOLS.) by E.C. Dargan

THE SHORTER CATECHISM ILLUSTRATED by John Whitecross

THE CHURCH MEMBER'S GUIDE by John Angell James

THE SUNDAY SCHOOL TEACHER'S GUIDE by John Angell James

THE DEVOTIONAL LIFE OF THE SS TEACHER by J.R. Miller

And several more....

Call us Toll Free at **1-877-666-9469**

Visit us on the web at **http://solid-ground-books.com**

Ric Ergenbright Titles

The beautiful photograph that graces the cover of this volume of Louis Berkhof was taken by Ric Ergenbright, a man who rejoices in the sovereign grace of God. He has published several volumes that combine the beauty of God's creation with the glory of His Word. We are delighted to offer the following for sale:

The Art of God

This award winning volume has been useful all over the world in spreading the glory of God's saving grace. Ric gives the story of God's grace in his life which is the backdrop of this breathtaking volume.

Think About These Things

This is the second volume in the *Art of God* trilogy, and in the words of John Piper, *"Here you will find (as always with Ric Ergenbright) the art of God wrapped in the Word of God."*

The Image of God

This is the third and final volume of the *Art of God* trilogy. This time Ric turns his camera to people, created in the image of God. People from all over the world are portrayed here with Scripture illuminating each photo.

Reflections

This is a devotional book unlike any you have seen. It takes Scripture, hymns and beautiful photography and leads you to see God, His world and His Word in a new way. There is room given for you to write down what you have learned that can be passed down to your posterity.

The Mercy of God and the Misery of Job

Ric joins his unique gift with John Piper to bring home the message of Job in a new and creative way. This book not only contains the words of Piper and the photos of Ergenbright, but it also has a cd of the book read by John Piper as well. This book will help you understand both the mercy of God and the misery of Job in new and profound ways.

Please visit his beautiful web site at **ricergenbright.com**

Printed in the United Kingdom
by Lightning Source UK Ltd.
106074UKS00001B/142-150